Insults! Insults!
BY "THE MOMA FACTORY"

The Best 400+ Insults/Jokes on the Planet (Uncensored & Censored)
2nd Edition

Insults! Insults! 2nd Edition

Table of Contents

Introduction 3

Chapter 1 – One Liner Insults................................ 4

Chapter 2 – Under the Belt Insults 9

Chapter 3 – Insults for Men, Women and
Relationships 20

Chapter 4 – Stereotype Insults 26

Chapter 5 – Handling Insults 29

Chapter 6 – "Yo Momma" Insults........................ 32

Chapter 7 – Technical Insults 35

Chapter 8 – Subtle Insults 42

Chapter 9 – Free For All 45

Chapter 10 – Sex and Crude Insults..................... 50

Chapter 11 – Learn from the Best: Insults from
Famous People...52

Chapter 12 – Bonus! Exotic and One-Word
Insults..55

Conclusion 69

Check Out My Other Books.................................. 70

Insults! Insults! 2nd Edition

Introduction

I want to thank you and congratulate you for purchasing the book, *"Insults! Insults! The Best 150 Insults/Jokes on the Planet (uncensored & censored)"*.

This book contains proven steps and strategies on how to become a master with the art of insults.

Here is a collection of the most irritating one-liners, insulting remarks, funniest insults, and clever comebacks to be used for annoying people.

Thanks again for purchasing this book, I hope you enjoy it!

Insults! Insults! 2nd Edition

Chapter 1 – One Liner Insults

Gone are the days when formality and manners are mandatory. Today, a person's communication skills and charisma are highly dependent in his sense of humor. It may sound crazy, but jokes and insults are *effective* ways to gain control of social situations, but they must also be used with responsibility.

With this being said, there has got to be a reason why you want to learn insults, but remember that your reason should never be to make someone else feel miserable; at least *not for a very long time.*

People use insults and jokes all the time. There are even social events arranged specifically so that people can throw insults at each other for entertainment. You may not necessarily be aiming to participate in such events, but insults can still be used to shut someone down. They can also lighten up dull and boring situations if used properly.

Insults for Arrogant People

Everybody hates egoistic people who think they know everything. Despite your efforts to talk some sense into them, it seems that any form of logic can't get past through their thick skulls. To start the first chapter of this book, here is a list of *one-liner insults* to be used for annoying people: (WARNING: Some words found in these insults may not be suitable for more sensitive people)

1. *Did you know that your birth certificate is an apology letter from a condom company?*

2. *I would like to ask how old you are, but even I can tell you can't really count that high.*

Insults! Insults! 2nd Edition

3. *I guess if assholes could fly, then this place must be an airport.*

4. *I don't really hate you, but if ever you were on fire and I had water, I'd drink it.*

5. *I'd like to see things in your perspective, but I can't stick my head too far up my ass.*

6. *If ever I decide to kill myself, I'd climb your ego and jump down to your IQ.*

7. *Stop thinking that everyone is your equal; you're offending a lot of people.*

8. *A lot of people live and learn; you just live.*

9. *I understand your point, but I still think you're full of shit.*

10. *Go right ahead and tell us everything you know; it'll probably take less than 10 seconds anyway.*

11. *Calling you stupid is insulting for stupid people.*

12. *Were you born stupid or did you work for it?*

13. *I'd ask your age but I doubt you can count that high*

14. *You didn't fall off the stupid tree; you got dragged through dumbass forest.*

15. *You couldn't hit water if you fell off a boat.*

16. *A halfwit gave you a piece of his mind, and you held on to it.*

17. *Are you brain-dead?*

18. *Keep talking, someday you'll say something intelligent!*

Insults! Insults! 2nd Edition

19. *Keep talking. I always yawn when I'm interested.*

20. *I have a brother who weighs 45 pounds – his weight is your IQ.*

21. *You're so stupid, brain surgeons are having a hard time locating your brain!*

22. *You're so stupid you tried to put M&Ms in alphabetical order!*

23. *The world is already full of idiots without you adding to it.*

24. *Brains aren't everything. In your case, they're nothing!*

25. *I think it's better for you to let someone to think you are an idiot rather than to open your mouth and prove them right.*

26. *Oh sorry, you've probably mistaken me for someone who gives a fuck.*

27. *Oh look, it's so cute! It knows how to talk!*

28. *I don't think you're stupid – but then, what's my single opinion compared to those of thousands of others?*

29. *You will never be the man that your mother used to be.*

30. *How about a nice warm cup of shut the fuck up?*

31. *Tell me; what part of this conversation leads you to believe that I give a fuck?*

32. *You remind me of myself; back when I was young and incredibly stupid.*

33. *Please, don't stop talking and maybe someday you'll actually say something intelligent.*

34. *Do you still love nature despite all it did to you?*

35. *Congratulations! You've proved that evolution can go backwards!*

36. *It's too bad that stupidity is not painful.*

37. *I have no idea what makes you incredibly stupid; but hey, it works!*

38. *I'd like to slap you but animal rights activists might sue me for animal abuse.*

39. *You're as strong as an ox and almost as intelligent.*

40. *I bet your brain is expensive since it was hardly used.*

41. *Your mind is like a steel trap – it's always closed!*

42. *I'd like to joke about your stupidity, but it'll take a whole day for you to figure it out.*

43. *Look, if I wanted to hear from an ass, I'll just fart.*

These are the insults that you can suddenly use to catch an annoying person off-guard. Of course, you should know when to execute these insults properly, and wait for the right time to strike.

The insults listed above are also great ways to end a losing conversation. But make sure you do so in a light manner and end it with a laugh, or else it will make you look like a sore loser. Of course, it can easily be used to make annoying people shut up.

Smart People

Insults! Insults! 2nd Edition

Sometimes, smart people also need to be taken down a peg or two, just so they'd stop being smug about being the smartest person in the room. Of course, if they leave themselves open for the following insults – then they're not really that smart. Here's how you win against the 'smarter' opponent!

44. *You occasionally stumble over the truth, but you quickly pick yourself up and carry on as if nothing happened.*

45. *I'm not going to waste my time teaching you something you couldn't be bothered to learn yourself.*

46. *Come again when you can't stay quite so long.*

47. *There's a tree somewhere that tirelessly produces oxygen so you can breathe. I think you should apologize to it.*

48. *I wish you no harm, but it would have been much better if you had never lived.*

49. *Well I could agree with you, but then we'd both be wrong.*

50. *You act like your arrogance is a virtue.*

51. *Some people bring happiness wherever they go; you bring happiness whenever you go.*

Chapter 2 – Under the Belt Insults

Basic Rule of Insulting

Before trying out any of the insults you will find in this book, keep in mind that you should only do so if this person is one of your best friends, or if this person is completely arrogant, annoying, or obnoxious.

If you have any form of decency, you would probably think that insulting someone too much for their superficial qualities might affect your maturity. But sometimes, we meet some people who truly deserve them. When someone is simply too annoying to put down lightly, it's time to bring out the big guns. Don't worry about being too personal, they'll get over it in time anyway.

Finally, there is a big difference between a regular person trying to insult someone and an all-out bully. And remember that no one likes bullies, so don't be one.

Insults for Fat People

There's really no reason to hate people just because of their weight. Being fat should not be something to insult someone about. However, sometimes being fat doesn't prevent some people from becoming annoying. So, when you encounter these situations, don't be afraid to use some of the following lines against them:

52. *Did you know that they made a song about your weight? 8675309!*

53. *Are you thinking what I'm thinking? No, it's not about food* (any name of food works).

54. *You're fat – don't sugarcoat it because you'll eat that too.*

Insults! Insults! 2nd Edition

55. *Hey, you have something on your chin – 3rd one down*

56. *You're so fat that if I took a photo of you last year, it'd still be printing today.*

57. *Stop insulting fat people – they already have enough on their plates.*

58. *You're so fat, when you stepped on a scale, your phone number appeared!*

59. *You're so fat, you leave footprints on concrete!*

60. *You're so fat; you need cheat codes just to play Wii Fit!*

61. **You:** *Dude, you're so fat!* **Fatty:** *Yeah, it runs in the family.* **You:** *Dude, no one runs in your family.*

62. *You're so fat that if I was watching TV and you walked in front of me, I'd miss 4 seasons of "insert TV show name here".*

63. *You're so fat that when you jumped into the ocean, whales started singing "We are family!"*

64. *You're so fat, they had to grease the door and put a Twinkie on the other side just so you can get through!*

65. *You're so fat that when you'd go to school, you'll be sitting next to everybody!*

66. *You're so fat, if you weighed at least 5 more pounds, you can actually get group insurance!*

67. *Do you remember the last time you saw your whole body in a mirror?*

Insults! Insults! 2nd Edition

68.   *You're so fat that when you stepped on the scale, it said "to be continued".*

69.   *If you'd go on a diet, there will be enough food to feed third-world countries.*

70.   *You're so fat that you wear two watches because your entire body covers two time zones!*

Insults for Skinny People

Of course, let's not forget the other end of the spectrum with these skinny insults!

71.   *You're so skinny you probably wipe your ass with floss.*

72.   *You're so skinny that if we put you on a flagpole, you'd wave in the wind.*

73.   *You're so skinny, you can dodge raindrops.*

74.   *The Olsen twins called – they want their eating disorder back.*

75.   *I would cut your throat out, but you need it to barf up your meals.*

76.   *I've seen more meat on a chicken!*

77.   *You're so skinny your nipples are hugging each other!*

78.   *You're so skinny you can use band-aids as maxi-pads.*

79.   *You're so skinny you disappear when you turn sideways!*

80. *You're so skinny your mom actually enjoyed your birth!*

Insults for Stupid People

The best way to insult arrogant people is to question their intelligence. Whether you're trying to put down a know-it-all jerk or insulting someone just for your own pleasure, you're going to need your own ammunition of clever lines; something *really mean.*

81. *You're so stupid that you were fired from the M&M's factory for throwing out all the "W's".*

82. *You started with nothing and still have most of it left.*

83. *You're so stupid that you thought a "quarterback" is a refund.*

84. *What drugs are you on, stupid pills?*

85. *Take off your hat, oh wait, that's your stupid hair!*

86. *I thought the wizard promised to give you a brain?*

87. *I don't know what makes you stupid – but it really works!*

88. *You're so stupid you got hit by a car. It was parked.*

89. *Everyone has the right to be stupid – but you're abusing the privilege.*

90. *Well, it looks like I overestimated the number of your brain cells.*

Insults! Insults! 2nd Edition

91. *If you would have twice the IQ you already have, you'd still be a moron.*

92. *You're so stupid; you climbed over a glass wall just so you can see the other side.*

93. *If stupidity is a disease, you'd probably be dead by now.*

94. *Yeah, I could agree with you, but then we'd both be idiots.*

95. *Are you always this stupid, or only when I'm around?*

96. *You're so dumb; you tripped over a cordless phone!*

97. *Surprise me; say something intelligent.*

98. *Are you sure you weren't born on the highway? Cause that's where most accidents happen.*

99. *Yeah, I can be nicer if you were any smarter.*

Insults for Ugly People

There's nothing wrong about being ugly; except if an ugly person is incredibly annoying or arrogant. When in doubt, here are several lines to put ugly people back to where they belong.

100. *If I had your face, I'd probably sue my parents.*

101. *Wow, I never knew shit could grow legs and walk.*

Insults! Insults! 2nd Edition

102. *I thought of you all day; I was at the zoo.*

103. *Why would I need a pet when I have you?*

104. *It looks like your face caught on fire and someone tried to put it out with a pitchfork.*

105. *You're so ugly that when your mom dropped you off at school, she got a fine for littering.*

106. *You look like what a pig and elephant's child would look like.*

107. *You're so ugly, apes want to adopt you.*

108. *We all sprang from apes, but you didn't spring far enough.*

109. *Is that your face or did your neck just throw up?*

110. *Seeing a face like yours, I wish I was blind.*

111. *I heard your parents took you to an ugly dog contest...and you won.*

112. *Oh my god, what happened to your face...oh, you're always like that.*

113. *Your face is the reason why God abandoned us.*

114. *Whatever it is you're eating, stop.*

115. *You have an old soul and it shows on your face.*

116. *The gene pool really did a number on you.*

117. *Here put this mask on so we can eat.*

118. *There's nothing wrong about being ugly; don't be sad.*

119. *Earlier today, I saw something that reminded me of you. Yeah, I flushed it and everything's back to normal.*

120. *Your face is something only a mother could love.*

121. *You're living proof that ugly people can still have sex.*

122. *If it's true that laughter is the best medicine, then you should show your face in hospitals more often.*

123. *You're so ugly that even Hello Kitty said goodbye to you.*

124. *When you were born, you were so ugly that the doctor threw you out the window; but the window threw you back!*

125. *Your face is the reason why men beat their wives.*

126. *Can I borrow your face? My ass is away on vacation.*

127. *You are the living proof Snow White and Dopey had sexual intercourse.*

128. *Aren't you supposed to be in Notre Dame ringing church bells?*

129. *Dude, your teeth are so yellow that when you smile, cars slow down.*

130. *If I were you, I'd kill myself.*

For Good Looking People

The good news is that good looking people are still worthy of insults – you just have to know exactly where to hit! Aside

Insults! Insults! 2ⁿᵈ Edition

from using the 'stupid' insults against them, you can also try ripping off their egos with the following criticisms!

131. *Maybe if you ate some of that makeup you could be pretty on the inside.*

132. *Being around you is like having a cancer of the soul.*

133. *Wow, you're even dumber than you look.*

134. *Beauty is skin deep, but ugly is to the bone.*

135. *Too bad your attitude doesn't match your face.*

136. *My personality dies a slow agonizing death when I talk to you.*

137. *Love to look at you; hate to listen to you.*

138. *Your boyfriend/girlfriend sure as hell isn't with you for your brains.*

139. *Do people really fall for you... despite who you are?*

140. *Are you this vapid because you spend all your time in front of the mirror?*

141. *I thought you were attractive, but then you opened your mouth.*

142. *You do realize makeup isn't going to fix your personality, right?*

Insults for Tall/Small People

143. *I won't make fun of your height – I wouldn't stoop that low.*

Insults! Insults! 2nd Edition

144.   Why don't you pick on someone your own size, like, the Eiffel Tower!

145.   You're so short you'll need to stand on a chair to reach puberty.

146.   Which one of the dwarves are you?

147.   You're so short that when it rains, you're the last one to know.

148.   You're so short you'd drown before you realize it was raining.

149.   You're so short if you pulled your socks up you won't be able to see.

150.   How's the weather down there?

Insults for Poor People

151.   You're so poor, when you went to a charity shop you asked when the sales are on.

152.   You're so poor you should be sponsored by a kid in Africa.

153.   You're so poor, I lit a match and the roaches ran out singing.

154.   You're so poor you don't even have enough money to pay attention.

155.   You're so poor, your version of cable TV is to go outside, watch the police and call it "Cops."

156.   You're so poor, even the Mexicans make fun of you!

Insults! Insults! 2nd Edition

157. *You're so poor that when I asked if I could use the bathroom you gave me two sticks, one for holding up the ceiling and another to swat the roaches with.*

158. *You're so poor you're always talking about the time you almost ate at a restaurant!*

159. *You're so poor that when I went to the bathroom in your home, a roach tripped me and a rat took my cash.*

160. *There was something about you that I liked, but you spent it.*

161. *You're so poor that when you go to McDonalds, you have to put the dollar meal on layaway!*

162. *You're so poor that if you didn't have a hard on when Christmas came, you wouldn't have anything to play with.*

163. *You're so poor that yesterday I saw your mother moving a trash can from one street to another. I asked what she was doing and she said, "I am moving my house to another place; it's too noisy out there!"*

Insults for Social Media Websites

Even the best insults can be worthless if they are done without an audience. Thanks to social media, an insult can potentially reach thousands or even millions of people. Let's face it, cyberbullying exists. It is possible that there may be a time when cyberbullying is completely abolished, but as long as it's still there, you might as well use cyberbullying against the cyberbullies themselves.

164. **1 Like = 1 Prayer** – this simple quote can be copy-pasted to any annoying photo of people who

Insults! Insults! 2nd Edition

thinks they're so beautiful, even though the whole world disagrees. '1 like = 1 prayer' is what you can commonly Just a reminder, insults are best made for people who are bullies themselves. It is also a nice comeback for someone who has been bashing you all this time.

165.   **Use 'memes'** – Internet 'memes' are photos, usually with a caption, that can be both funny and insulting at the same time. There are already hundreds of popular memes being used in social media websites, but anyone can still come up with their own using a funny photo and a website that allows users to create their own memes.

Most of the insults in this book can still be just as effective in social media websites as with physical confrontations. Just remember to use the appropriate insult for the appropriate situation, and with the appropriate person.

Chapter 3 – Insults for Men, Women and Relationships

Insults for your Ex

Want to make your ex feel like the biggest loser for breaking up with you? Here's how!

166.	*You want my ass? You had my ass; you let my ass walk away. The only ass left is your dumb ass!*

167.	*Marriage is like a hot bath – once you get used to it, it's not so hot.*

168.	*I heard you were dating my ex – how do I taste?*

169.	*I'm only keeping your number so I know not to answer when you call.*

170.	*Please, my battery lasts longer than your relationship.*

171.	*He probably fucks around because he needs the practice.*

172.	*Marriage is like a midnight phone call. First there's the ring, THEN you wake up.*

173.	*You're like the first slice of bread – you get touched by everyone, but no one really wants you.*

174.	*Don't be sad about being alone on Valentine's Day. After all, nobody loves you the rest of the year either.*

175.	**Ex:** *You'll never find someone like me.* **You:** *That's the point.*

Insults! Insults! 2nd Edition

176.   *I never forget the first time we met, although I'll keep trying.*

177.   *Women might be able to fake orgasms, but men can fake entire relationships.*

178.   *I wish our marriage certificate came with an expiration date.*

179.   *I've had many cases of love that were just infatuation, but this hate I feel for you is the real thing.*

180.   *Roses are red, violets are blue. Garbage is dumped, and so are you.*

181.   *Wanna get laid? Just crap up a chicken's ass and wait!*

182.   *They say opposites attract – so that must mean you'll meet someone good looking, cultured, and intelligent.*

Comebacks for Girls

Face the facts; girls can sometimes be even more annoying than boys. What's more annoying is that some girls will always think they are better than you no matter what. If this is the case, then there's nothing more satisfying than telling them something they will never forget.

183.   *The smartest thing that ever came out of your mouth was a dick.*

184.   *She has a nice butter face. Everything looks nice, except her face.*

185.   *And, that's the reason why women earn 75 cents to the dollar.*

Insults! Insults! 2nd Edition

186. *Aww; you're cute when you talk about things you don't understand.*

187. *You're not pretty enough to be that much of a bitch.*

188. *She thinks the car's rear-view is for putting on make-up.*

189. *Somebody call animal control – we've got a stray bitch running around!*

190. *Please tell me you don't home-school your kids.*

191. *Her mouth's dirtier than a wicker toilet seat.*

192. *You better hope you marry rich.*

193. *She's got a body that won't quit and a brain that won't start.*

194. *She's a lot like train tracks - she's been laid across the country.*

195. *You're so fake Barbie is more real than you.*

196. *I could remove 90% of your beauty with a tissue.*

197. *The only thing that goes erect when I'm near you is my middle finger.*

198. *What are you doing out of the kitchen?*

199. *If you're going to be two-faced, you should at least make one of them pretty.*

200. *How much semen did you swallow to become that stupid?*

201. *You wouldn't wear shoes if you didn't have any feet, so why are you wearing a bra?*

Insults! Insults! 2nd Edition

202. *I called your boyfriend gay and he hit me with his purse!*

203. *They call it PMS because Mad Cow Disease was already taken.*

204. *If you ever become a mother, can I have one of the puppies?*

Comebacks for Guys

205. *For a guy, you have really huge tits!*

206. *I heard you were a lady-killer. They take one look at you and they die of shock!*

207. *You're just made because your hair is straighter than you are.*

208. *I'd love to go out with you but my favorite commercial is on.*

209. *You know what they say about guys with big muscles: [pause for effect] small dicks.*

210. *I'd rather throw a puppy in a wood chipper than talk to you.*

211. *Bitch some more and I'd start thinking it's that time of the month.*

212. *Wow, what a car! You must be <u>really</u> compensating for something (look at his crotch sadly)*

213. *All I heard was, "Blah blah blah, I'm an asshole."*

214. *For a minute there I thought you were complaining about your sore vagina.*

215. *Hold on, I'll go find you a tampon.*

Insults! Insults! 2nd Edition

216. *Guys are like parking spots. All the good ones are taken, and the rest are handicapped.*

217. *Your wife said she liked seafood – so I gave her crabs.*

218. *A demitasse would fit his head like a sombrero.*

219. *Man alive! But I wish you weren't.*

220. *I've been warned men with small dicks like to talk a lot. I see what they mean.*

221. *He doesn't know the meaning of the word fear, but then again he doesn't know the meaning of most words.*

222. *Its men like you that turn women gay.*

223. *You loud Dick-Lips*

224. *I heard you're happily married – but your wife isn't.*

225. *Life is short and so is your penis.*

226. *I wouldn't fuck you for practice.*

227. *If I had balls, they would be bigger than yours.*

228. *Look, you grew a pube...wait, that's just your dick.*

229. *Your dick is so small it could floss teeth.*

230. *I'm not your type – I'm not inflatable.*

231. *My heels are bigger than your dick.*

232. *If you were any more of a dick, gay guys would be sucking your forehead.*

233. *You're the big dick you'll never have.*

Insults! Insults! 2nd Edition

234.   You're better at sex than anyone – now if only you could find a partner.

Chapter 4 – Stereotype Insults

Insulting someone for their ethnicity, skin, or hair color is nothing new. Although most of these insults and racisms can be too harsh, sometimes you have to play dirty if this person truly deserves it. Just remember that all of these insults are mostly untrue and you should always think *twice* before using them.

WARNING: In today's society, racism is unacceptable. To use the following insults properly, make sure that the person you're using them on truly deserves it. Otherwise, it can be used as *unreal insults* (between two best friends, brothers, etc.) for good laughs. Here are some of the best insults for the most common stereotypes in today's society:

Insults for Blondes

There are many stereotypes that target blonde people. Interestingly, most of these stereotypes specifically target blonde girls. Blonde female or not, here are some of the best insults for blondes:

235. *Just because you're blonde doesn't mean you should act like an idiot.*

236. *Way to reinforce stereotypes.*

237. **Ask:** *How can you confuse a blonde?* **Answer:** *You can't; they're born that way.*

238. **Ask:** *What's the difference between a blonde girl and a pit bull?* **Answer:** *Lipstick.*

239. *You're pretty; pretty (fucking) stupid.*

240. *No amount of hair dye will ever fix this much level of stupid.*

Insults! Insults! 2nd Edition

241. *It's a good thing that hair color is not contagious.*

242. **Ask:** *Do you know what happens when a blonde person gets Alzheimer's?* **Answer:** *Her IQ increases.*

243. *Don't be lost in thought; you'd probably be a total stranger there.*

244. **Ask:** *What do you call a blonde person in a library?* **Answer:** *Lost.*

245. *Oh sweetie, take some of your dad's money and buy yourself some personality.*

Jokes/Insults for African-Americans

Be very careful and responsible when insulting people based on their skin color. Not only can some of them be extremely sensitive when their ethnicity is put into play, it's also not a very nice thing to do to use such insults in an argument; even for jokes. The best thing would be to use these insults if *you are with the same skin color,* otherwise, be decent and forget using the following insults. Finally, remember that making racist remarks is only acceptable if it is the only way to deal with absolutely obnoxious people, or for two good friends looking for some laughs.

246. **Ask:** *What's black and yellow, and makes you laugh?* **Answer:** *A bus filled with black dudes going over a cliff.*

247. **Ask:** *How would you know if a black person has been using your computer?* **Answer:** *It's not there anymore.*

248. **Ask:** *What is incredibly long and hard for a black dude?* **Answer:** *1st grade.*

Insults! Insults! 2nd Edition

249. **Ask:** *What's the difference between a white person and a black person telling a fairytale?* **Answer:** *The white person starts with "Once upon a time", while the black person starts with "y'all motherfuckers ain't gonna believe dis shit!"*

250. **Ask:** *What do you call a black man in a suit?* **Answer:** *Defendant.*

Asian Insults/Jokes (Mostly *Chinese*)

For stereotypes; if you're Asian, then you're probably Chinese. Obviously, this is not true, but any insult intended for Chinese people can work for any Asian as well. Just like before, remember that insults targeting someone's race should only be for *humor* and not for real confrontations intended to humiliate or degrade.

251. **Ask:** *What do Asians do during erections?* **Answer:** *They vote.*

252. **Ask:** *What is the name of an Asian billionaire?* **Answer:** *Cha Ching!*

253. **Ask:** *How can you put a blindfold on an Asian person?* **Answer:** *Use floss.*

254. **Just call them:** *Jackie Chan.*

Chapter 5 – Handling Insults

In today's society, it is virtually impossible to live a live without being insulted. Social media websites and today's television do little to lessen the occurrences of these insults, so you might as well learn how to deal with them.

Insults are only guaranteed to be funny unless they are targeting you. You can also build your tolerance for such insults, but it's much better to respond with *comebacks*.

Eventually, someone will be trying to insult you. However, it is easy to get the insult right back at them especially if they have no idea you were reading this book.

Comeback Situations

The best way to respond from insults is to make insults themselves. There is nothing more satisfying than teaching an idiot that they shouldn't mess with you. Basically, you should be prepared with comebacks from the most common insults heading your way.

If Someone Calls You Fat

Besides saying "thank you!" which a lot of insulters hate, you can also try:

255.   *I may be fat; but you're ugly and I could still lose weight.*

If Someone Insults You

To be good with insults, you should also know how to take insults. Still, knowing comeback phrases is not enough to be effective in handling insults. You should also be able to control your temper, take some time to practice, and remember to laugh and have fun.

256. *Wow, how long did it take you to come up with that?*

257. *Yeah, I could probably eat a bowl of alphabet soup and crap out a better statement than that.*

258. *If you wanted to be a smartass, you should first be smart; otherwise you'll only be an ass.*

259. *I bet you stayed up all night coming up with that statement.*

260. *Boo hoo, I feel really bad now. Please shut the fuck up.*

261. *Wow, here's a two thumbs up ... your ass.*

262. *Um, okay. What am I supposed to feel?*

263. *Thank you for confirming that there really are idiots in the world.*

264. **When someone tries to insult you:** *Open your mouth, eyes, and nostrils as wide as you can and stare back at him/her.*

Comebacks for Old People

Basically, it is never right to insult your elderly. In fact, it's never right to insult anyone at all. Being able to respect people the same way you want to be respected yourself is a true indication of maturity. But it is also true that respect should be earned, and is not a free privilege for older people.

Insults! Insults! 2nd Edition

If ever you are faced with an obnoxious senior (or just someone who is older than you), here are several lines you could try:

265. *Yeah, you're so old your farts are dust.*

266. *Yeah, you're so old; your birth certificate is expired.*

267. *You're so old; you probably remember when the Dead Sea was still just feeling ill.*

268. *You're so old that even your teeth have wrinkles!*

Finally, throwing insults in response to another insult can have dire effects on your personality and relationships, unless it is all a joke. Learning about insults is a good idea of fun, but don't expect to develop your communications skills with insults.

Insults! Insults! 2nd Edition

Chapter 6 – "Yo Momma" Insults

Also referred to as "maternal insults", "Yo Momma" insults became a popular way to offend or ridicule someone by insulting that person's mother. Interestingly, a Yo Momma insult is often followed by another Yo Momma insult from the target. Usually, this cycle goes on with the exchange of Yo Momma insults from both persons until there is a distinct winner; usually decided by the spectators.

To make sure you are equipped for such a confrontation, it is ideal to make your own insults since most of the good ones get overused quickly. However, coming up with your own Yo Momma joke can be very difficult and not a lot can come up with good ones. Hence, here are some of the best Yo Momma insults for your reference.

269.   *Yo Momma's so stupid; she tried waking up a sleeping bag.*

270.   *Yo Momma's so stupid; she tried to buy tickets for Xbox Live!*

271.   *Yo Momma's so old; she went with Moses during 3rd grade.*

272.   *Yo Momma's so ugly, she really has to be your momma.*

273.   *Yo Momma's so dumb that she sits on your TV to watch the couch.*

274.   *Yo Momma's so old that her social security number is 000-00-0001.*

275.   *Yo Momma's so old that when she went to an antiques auction, people started bidding on her.*

Insults! Insults! 2nd Edition

276. *Yo Momma's so dumb; she tried to steal a free sample.*

277. *Yo Momma's so dumb; she stared at an orange juice for an hour because it says "concentrate".*

278. *Yo Momma's so ugly that she makes blind people cry!*

279. *Yo Momma's so ugly that your dad takes her to work so he doesn't have to kiss her goodbye.*

280. *Yo Momma's so (fucking) ugly, people dressed up as her for Halloween!*

281. *Yo Momma's so hideous, when she went to the pool, all the water went out!*

282. *Yo Momma's so ugly that she makes onions cry!*

283. *Yo Momma's so ugly that she got fired from a "blow job".*

284. *Yo Momma's so fat and stupid; the only letters in the alphabet she knows are KFC!*

285. *Yo Momma's so poor, she can't even pay attention!*

286. *Yo Momma's smells so bad, North Korea wants to use her as a chemical weapon!*

287. *Yo Momma's so stupid that she brought a spoon to the Superbowl!*

288. *Yo Momma's so dumb that she tried selling your car to get money for gas.*

289. *Yo Momma's so fat that they even had to change "One Size Fits All" to "One Size Fits Most".*

Insults! Insults! 2nd Edition

290. *Yo Momma's so stupid that she went to a Clippers game to get a haircut.*

291. *Yo Momma's so dumb that she tried to kill a fish by drowning it.*

292. *Yo Momma's so ugly that she gave Chuck Norris a heart attack!*

293. *Yeah, you can look like your mother...if you'd grow a beard...and gain a few thousand pounds.*

Insults! Insults! 2nd Edition

Chapter 7 – Technical Insults

Some people are naturally born with the ability to give insults masterfully. Here is the truth; giving insults is a skill, and although it may come naturally for some people, it can still be acquired through practice.

To some people, insults are a form of art. It takes real charisma and people skills to pull off insults with fluency and success. This means that before you go around and start insulting everybody you see; make sure you've already developed your communication skills.

Before giving insults, pay attention to these two things:

Crowd – Take note of the audience when attempting to insult someone. Will they take your side, or the person you will insult? Do you see some of your friends around? Also try to assess the reaction of the crowd o the person you are about to insult. If the crowd is already annoyed with this person, then you're more likely to succeed. Although you no longer have to pay attention to the crowd in one-on-one confrontations, remember that there is power in numbers.

Timing - Timing is also important if you want to execute an insult properly. Obviously, you shouldn't suddenly fire an insult on someone out of the blue. Each social situation is unique, and there is no definite formula to identify the perfect timing to give insults. As a general rule, try to give an insult in moments when you will be heard clearly. Basically, avoid speaking over a noisy crowd or any loud noise.

Exit – Ending your insult is just as important as the execution. After a successful insult, enjoy the reaction of the crowd and just smile. Be ready for a comeback from your target, but you can easily walk away and end the confrontation victoriously.

Tips for Insults

Good insults cannot be given just by anyone. Your charisma, and the way you present yourself during, after, and before an insult is important for determining the outcome. Here are some tips to help you give insults with confidence:

1. **Make sure to use insults that made you laugh.** This book contains 150 insults and jokes, but this doesn't mean that you should use all of them. A tip for insulting with confidence is to use only the ones that made you smile or laugh the first time you read them.

2. **Practice showing some attitude.** Your attitude is what makes insults more believable. How else do you expect someone to take your insults seriously without attitude?

3. **Try to avoid crowds in which you're sure to lose.** Make it a habit to always be with your friends. This way, you will be less likely to be a target of insults while increasing the efficacy of the insults you will be making yourself.

4. **Accept defeat like a champ.** Remember that insults should be something anyone shouldn't take seriously. When you feel like defeat is imminent, just laugh it off, smile, and resume doing what you were doing before.

Shakespearean Insults

An interesting thing about insults is the more unique they are, the more they seem to work. It is true that any person can come up with a new insult, but if it's *that good,* suddenly everyone is using it.

Creating good insults takes intelligence and a good play on words, so it is only natural that a literary genius can create great insults that can stand the test of time.

Also keep in mind that these insults may work better in social media websites, since saying things like these in person may sound ridiculous. They are also particularly interesting to use when talking to a friend.

294. *"Villain, I have done thy mother."* – A classic way to say "I f*cked your mom".

295. *"Away, you three inch fool!"* – This is a classy way to insult the "length" of a man.

296. *"Thou art unfit for any place but hell."* – More annoying if your target is ugly and religious at the same time.

297. *"More of your conversation would affect my brain."* – This is a good remark if you have been trying to talk some sense into someone but they seem mentally incapable to understand.

298. *"Thou art the son & heir of a mongrel bitch."* – Again, the classic way of saying "son of a bitch".

299. *"A fusty nut with no kernel."* – This phrase can have two meanings; either someone offers nothing on the inside (probably intelligence), or someone lacking an essential quality to be complete.

Witty / Clever Insults

Finally, if you want to be good with insults, you should know how to use clever remarks for various situations. Here are some witty, sarcastic insults for you to practice with.

Insults! Insults! 2nd Edition

300. **When someone says:** *"Wanna hear a joke?"* **You say:** *"Nah, you're already a joke by yourself."*

301. **When someone says:** *"I feel so stupid."* **You say:** *"Yeah, we know"* or *"Well, it's a good thing you're honest."*

302. **When someone says:** *"Why can't I do this?"* **You say:** *"Maybe it's because of your genes."*

303. **When someone shows you his/her clothes and says:** *"How do I look?"* **You say:** *"It looks good, but not on you."*

304. **When someone asks you:** *"What do you think of me"* (or something similar). **You say:** *"Besides being irritating, stupid, ugly, and smelly, yeah, you're pretty okay."*

305. *If you stand close enough, I can hear the ocean.*

306. **When someone asks you to do something:** *"Oh, I'd love to! But I can't, I don't like you."*

307. *I'd love to stay and chat but I'd rather have Type 2 diabetes.*

308. *I wish I could but I don't want to.*

309. *If you're talking about me behind my back that just means my life is more interesting than yours.*

310. *Any similarity between you and a human is purely coincidental!*

311. *Careful now, don't let your brains go to your head!*

312. *Diarrhea of the mouth; constipation of the ideas.*

Insults! Insults! 2nd Edition

313. *Pardon me, but you've obviously mistaken me for someone who gives a damn.*

314. *Don't get insulted, but is your job devoted to spreading ignorance?*

315. *People say that you are the perfect idiot. I say that you are not perfect but you are doing all right.*

316. *As an outsider, what do you think of the human race?*

317. *Don't feel bad. A lot of people have no talent!*

318. *It's hard to get the big picture when you have such a small screen.*

319. *Did the mental hospital test too many drugs on you today?*

320. *Learn from your parents' mistakes - use birth control!*

321. *Judging by the old saying, "What you don't know can't hurt you," he's practically invulnerable.*

322. *Before you came along we were hungry. Now we are fed up.*

323. *Don't mind him. He has a soft heart and a head to match.*

324. *Don't let your mind wander -- it's too little to be let out alone.*

325. *Believe me, I don't want to make a monkey out of you. Why should I take all the credit?*

326. *I've come across decomposed bodies that are less offensive than you are.*

Insults! Insults! 2nd Edition

327.   Nobody says that you are dumb. They just say you were sixteen years old before you learned how to wave good-bye.

328.   Don't thank me for insulting you. It was my pleasure.

329.   Don't you have a terribly empty feeling ---- in your skull?

330.   So, a thought crossed your mind? Must have been a long and lonely journey.

331.   Go ahead, tell them everything you know. It'll only take 10 seconds.

332.   He is living proof that man can live without a brain!

333.   There is no vaccine against stupidity.

334.   The inbreeding is certainly obvious in your family.

335.   He is depriving a village somewhere of an idiot.

Remember that constantly making insults must be used with caution. Depending on the social situation, it can be frowned upon and be viewed as something immature. In short, try not to make insults to other people (except your friends) unless absolutely necessary.

Finally, remember that using a lot of insults in social situations may affect the way your personality is perceived by the people around you. Make sure that when you make insults, it is not obstructing progress and productivity.

Insults! Insults! 2nd Edition

Chapter 8 – Subtle Insults

They say the best insults are the ones where the people you're insulting don't even know they've been insulted. Of course – where's the fun in that? How would you enjoy the insult if others don't realize they've been insulted? Still, subtle insults are a fine thing to master – just in case you really, really want to target someone while in a public setting. Following are some subtle insults that you can try practicing!

336. *Are your parents first cousins?*

337. *You must be an acquired taste.*

338. *Slit your wrists - it will lower your blood pressure.*

339. *He's just visiting this planet.*

340. *Some folks are so dumb they have to be watered twice a week.*

341. *[Name] has reached rock bottom and is starting to dig.*

342. *[Name] forgot to pay his brain bill.*

343. *Too bad stupidity isn't painful.*

344. *When you die, I'd like to go to your funeral but I'll probably have to go to work that day. I believe in business before pleasure.*

345. *Somebody else is doing the driving for that boy!*

346. *He has a mechanical mind. Too bad he forgot to wind it up this morning.*

347. *The next time you shave, could you stand a little closer to the razor?*

Insults! Insults! 2nd Edition

348.

349.　*A guy with your IQ should have a low voice too!*

350.　*Let me guess... your parents didn't hug you enough as a kid.*

351.　*Talked to planktons lately?*

352.　*Do you remember eating paint chips when you were a kid?*

353.　*Look, don't go to a mind reader; go to a palmist; I know you've got a palm.*

354.　*A sharp tongue isn't synonymous with a keen mind.*

355.　*Do you ever wonder what life would be like if you'd had enough oxygen at birth?*

356.　*No one will ever know that you've had a lobotomy, if you wear a wig to hide to the scars and learn to control the slobbering.*

357.　*After meeting you, I no longer feel negatively about abortion, particular those involving cases of incest.*

358.　*All that you are you owe to your parents. Why don't you send them a penny and square the account?*

359.　*Alone: In bad company.*

360.　*And there he was: reigning supreme at number two.*

361.　*Keep talking – I always yawn when I'm interested.*

Insults! Insults! 2nd Edition

362. *You are down to earth, but not quite down enough.*

363. *I really wish we were better strangers.*

364. *I don't know what I did that offended you. Can you tell me what it is so I could do it again?*

365. *You could be the counter-argument for intelligent design.*

366. *The problem with you is that you lack the power of conversation but not the power of speech.*

367. *When someone gets cut, you cry over them just to get salt on the wound.*

368. *Are you a cutter? You should be.*

369. *What circle of hell are you from?*

370. *It won't be the same with you...it will be better.*

371. *You're a ground-hugger*

372. *If you really want to know about mistakes, you should ask your parents.*

373. *I was taught not to say anything if I can't say anything good, so...*

374. *I'm not insulting you – I'm describing you.*

375. *Why so quiet? Are you speaking your mind?*

376. *You have the sexual morals of a man.*

377. *Why don't you slip into something more comfortable...like a coma?*

378. *Save your breath, you'll need it to blow up your date tonight.*

Insults! Insults! 2nd Edition

379.   Unfortunately, stupidity is not a crime – so you're free to go.

380.   300 million sperm cells and you were the fastest?!

381.   The jerk store called, they're running out of you.

382.   Did your parents ever ask you to run away from home?

383.   **Person:** See you! **You:** Not if I see you first!

384.   You have a great face for makeup.

385.   The last time I saw something like you, I flushed it.

386.   When 3 people have sex it's called a threesome. When two people have sex it's called a twosome. Now I know why they call you HANDsome!

Chapter 9 – Free For All

Sometimes, you just can't classify an insult per category. In this Chapter, we're presenting you with a wide variety of insults – just pick the ones you like or the one that best fits your current situation!

387. *I regret some of the things I said last night. I came up with better insults this morning.*

388. *I've only got one nerve left, and you're getting on it.*

389. *Let's play horse. I'll be the front end and you be yourself.*

390. *At least you are not obnoxious like so many other people - you are obnoxious in a different and worse way!*

391. *I've seen people like you before – but I had to pay admission!*

392. *Make somebody happy – mind your own damn business!*

393. *Perhaps your whole purpose in life is to serve as a warning to others.*

394. *I'd slap you – but that would be animal abuse.*

395. *Your adult acne is ruining the party.*

396. *Your family tree is a cactus because everyone on it is a prick.*

397. *Why don't you shut up and give that hole on your face time to heal?*

Insults! Insults! 2nd Edition

398. *Do you have to leave so soon? I was just about to poison the tea.*

399. *You must have been born on the highway because that's where most accidents happen.*

400. *Two wrongs don't make a right – take your parents for example.*

401. *You're mom just called. She wanted you to pick up a loaf of bread, eggs, and some condoms – so she doesn't make the same mistake twice.*

402. *Here's 20 cents, call all your friends and give me back the change.*

403. *Why don't you check up on eBay to see if they have a life for sale?*

404. *I can eat a bowl of alphabet soup and crap out a better comeback than that!*

405. *The only positive about you is your HIV status.*

406. *You grow on people – like a wart.*

407. *You're as thick as poop but definitely not as useful.*

408. *I strongly advise you against breeding.*

409. *Better hide, the garbage collector is coming.*

410. *My love for you is like this scar – ugly but permanent.*

411. *You're the reason God created the middle finger.*

412. *You have an inferiority complex – and it's fully justified.*

Insults! Insults! 2nd Edition

413.   I never forget a face but in your case, I'll make an exception.

414.   You're not as bad as people say – you're actually worse.

415.   I heard the only place you've ever been invited is outside.

416.   When people see you, they clap. That is, they clap their hands over their eyes.

417.   Do you have to leave so soon? I was just about to poison your drink.

418.   I'm busy. Can I ignore you another time?

419.   You should do some soul searching – maybe you'll find one.

420.   You are cordially invited to go fuck yourself.

421.   I used to think you're an ass – now I have a lesser opinion of you.

422.   You bring out the best insults in me.

423.   Is that a scar?! Oh, it's just your mouth.

424.   Grip your ears firmly and pull it out of your ass!

425.   Oh, is it bitch-o-clock?

426.   Roses are red, violets are blue. I can honestly say, it sucks to be you.

427.   I'm sorry, I can't think of a non-insulting way to describe you.

428.   Stop editing your pictures so much! What if you go missing?

Insults! Insults! 2nd Edition

429. *Somehow after you shower, you look even greasier.*

430. *Did someone leave your cage open?*

431. *When you were born, not only did they break the mold – they shot the mold maker!*

432. *Someday you'll find yourself – and you'll wish you didn't.*

433. *I hate you. Maybe not in an "I hope you die" kind of way, rather "I hope you develop a fatal allergy to bacon and ice cream."*

434. *Twinkle twinkle little snitch, mind your own business you nosy bitch.*

435. *You started at the bottom, and it's been downhill ever since.*

436. *I heard you went to see the doctor to have a little wart removed – so he threw you out of the office!*

437. *I don't mind that you're talking as long as you don't mind that I'm not listening*

438. *Some people are has-beens. You're a never-was.*

439. *I think Mother Nature really hates you. You're a reminder of all her mistakes.*

440. *You remind me of the ocean – you make me sick!*

441. *I know you'd go to the end of the world for me – but would you stay there?*

442. *Is your name Maple Syrup? It should be – you sap.*

Insults! Insults! 2nd Edition

443. *My worst nightmare is that one day, someone might hate me as much as I hate you.*

444. *You add to, not diminish, pain!*

445. *There are already lots of people in the world to hate – do you have to be another one?*

446. *You look like something the cat dragged in.*

447. *Anyone who told you to be yourself gave you bad advice.*

448. *God loves you – but everyone else thinks you're a dick.*

449. *Don't worry; no one gives a shit what you think.*

450. *If God is real, then why are you here?*

451. *When I meet people like you, I realize why aliens don't want to introduce themselves.*

452. *Your mother is a hamster and your father smells of elderberry!*

Insults! Insults! 2nd Edition

Chapter 10 – Sex and Crude Insults

Of course, let's not forget the uncensored part of this book! Following are other crude and sexual insults that should leave someone properly insulted!

453. *Practice safe sex – go screw yourself.*

454. *Fuck you very much.*

455. *You got more issues than Playboy but not nearly as entertaining!*

456. *My kid knocked up your honor student.*

457. *How many times should I flush before I get rid of you?*

458. *That's a lovely shade of slut you're wearing today.*

459. *Your penis is so small it's a choking hazard.*

460. *I heard you were fired from the sperm bank for drinking on the job.*

461. *Twinkle twinkle little slut, you like dick inside your butt.*

462. *I'd punch you if I weren't so disgusted by your face.*

463. *I'd call you a cunt but you don't have the depth or the warmth.*

464. *Put some sand in your crotch, it will make the crabs feel at home.*

465. *You were supposed to be a stain on the carpet.*

466. *I would shove my foot up your ass, except you'd probably enjoy it.*

Insults! Insults! 2nd Edition

467. *Your mom should have swallowed.*

468. *You're why we have birth control.*

469. *Your dick is a landmine: small, hidden, and explodes on contact.*

470. *I bet your dad is regretting he didn't pull out.*

471. *You're such a huge turd, cats try to bury you.*

Chapter 11 – Learn from the Best: Insults from Famous People

Some of the best insults came from some of the brightest minds in history. You'll be amazed at how well-crafted these insults are and just how incredibly fast are their responses, making each insult even more valuable! Following are some of the best insults coming from famous people and the circumstances in which they were delivered. Read them, laugh out loud, and use variations of these insults whenever you're presented with the opportunity!

- *I've just learned about your illness, let's hope it's not something trivial – Irvin S. Cobb*

- *He is so old his blood type was discontinued – Bill Dana*

- *He can compress the most words into the smallest idea of anyone I know – Abraham Lincoln*

- *I won't insult your intelligence by suggesting that you really believe what you just said – William F. Buckley*

- *I didn't attend the funeral, but I sent a nice letter saying I approved of it – Mark Twain*

- *I am enclosing two tickets to the first night of my new play; bring a friend. If you have one – George Bernard Shaw to Churchill*

- *As useless as rubber lips on a woodpecker – Earl Pitts*

- *Cannot possibly attend first night, will attend second...if there is one – Churchill's response to Shaw*

- *He has delusions of adequacy – Walter Kerr*

Insults! Insults! 2nd Edition

- *As welcome as a rattlesnake on a square dance –
  Robert Reinhold*

- **Critics:** *We never want to look like you.* **Arnold
  Schwarzenegger:** *Don't worry, you never will. (in
  reference to his physique as a bodybuilder)*

- *I've had a perfectly wonderful evening, but this wasn't
  it – Groucho Marx*

- *He has Van Gogh's ear for music – Billy Wilder*

- *She speaks five languages and can't act in any of them
  – Sir John Gielgud*

- *Michael Jackson's album was called Bad because there
  wasn't enough room in the sleeve for Pathetic – Prince*

- *He has never been known to use a word that might
  send a reader to a dictionary – William Faulkner
  about Hemingway*

- *The easiest way for you (Elton John) to lose 10 pounds
  is just take off your wig - Madonna*

- *He has no enemies but is intensely disliked by his
  friends – Oscar Wilde*

- *He loves nature in spite of what it did to him – Forest
  Tucker*

- *There is nothing wrong with you that reincarnation
  won't cure – Jack E. Leonard*

- *He (Nixon) inherited some good instincts from his
  Quaker forbearers, but by diligent hard work, he
  overcame them – James Reston*

- *I have never killed a man, but I have read many
  obituaries with great pleasure – Clarence Darrow*

Insults! Insults! 2nd Edition

The Churchill Corner

Winston Churchill is praised for his many accomplishments in life. An incredibly smart man who went head to head with Hitler, Churchill was hailed one of the best wartime leaders during the 20th century. There are many tags to his name: United Kingdom Prime Minister, writer, Nobel Prize Literature Winner, and Witty Insult Savant. Here are just some of the best comebacks and one-liners from Churchill.

- *A modest man who has much to be modest about.*

- *Tell him I can only deal with one shit at a time. (when interrupted while at the toilet)*

- *I wish Stanley Baldwin no ill, but it would have been much better if he had never lived.*

- **Lady Astor:** *Winston, if you were my husband I would flavor your coffee with poison.* **Churchill:** *Madam, if I were you husband, I should drink it.*

- *An appeaser is one who feeds a crocodile hoping it would eat him last.*

- *He has all the virtues I dislike and none of the vices I admire.*

- **Bessie Braddock:** *Winston, you're drunk!* **Churchill:** *Bessie, you're ugly, and tomorrow morning I shall be sober.*

Insults! Insults! 2nd Edition

Chapter 12 – Bonus! Exotic and One-Word Insults

As you've probably figured out after reading the selection of insults, there's more than one way of delivering a set down on someone's face, body, skin, beliefs, intelligence, gender, age, and various other attributes. However, you might be surprised to find out that other cultures have their own brand of insults, some of them highly creative, intensely funny, and wonderfully insulting. Sure, the person you're insulting might not realize they're being insulted, but you will know and that will be enjoyment enough!

Ready? Here are some bonus insults you should definitely learn about and use as often as possible!

Roman Insults

Actual: *Sa-mi bagi mana-n cur si sa-mi faci laba la cacat*

Translation: *Stick your hand in my ass and jerk off with my shit.*

**

Actual: *Shampona-mi-ai flocii cu saliva*

Translation: *Shampoo my dick-hair with your saliva.*

**

Actual: *Futu-tzi coliva ma~tii*

Translation: *Fuck your mother's funeral meal.*

**

Actual: *Spala-te pe dinti ca vin cu pula inspectie*

Translation: *Brush your teeth, my dick will be inspecting soon!*

Danish Insult

Actual: *Sut djavlepik I helvede din bossedvarg*

Translation: *Suck devil cock in hell you faggot dwarf*

Finnish Insult:

Actual: *kuse muuntajaan*

Translation: *piss into a transformer*

Vietnamese Insult

Actual: *May an long dai cham mui*

Translation: *You eat pubic hair with salt dip*

Albanian Insult

Actual: *te qifte arusha qorre*

Translation: *May you get fucked by a blind bear*

Bosnia Insult

Actual: *Sanjam da prdnem na tebe*

Translation: *I dream about farting on you*

Afrikaans Insult

Actual: *Siug aan my aambeie en wag vir beter dae*

Translation: *Suck on my piles and just wait for more pleasant days*

Spanish Insults

Actual: *Chupe mantequilla de mi culo*

Translation: *Suck butter from my ass*

**

Actual: *Me cago en tus muertos*

Translation: *I shit on your dead*

**

Actual: *Me cago en Dios*

Translation: *I shit on God*

**

Actual: *Me cago en tu puta madre*

Translation: *I shit in/on your whore mother*

**

Actual: *Me cago en la leche*

Translation: *I shit in the milk*

Turkish Insult

Insults! Insults! 2nd Edition

Actual: *Sana girsin keman yayi*

Translation: *May the bow of a violin enter your anus*

Arabian Insults

Actual: *Elif air ab dinikh*

Translation: *A thousand dicks in your religion*

**

Actual: *Air il'e yoshmotak*

Translation: *May you be struck by a dick*

**

Actual: *Airy fe dameerak*

Translation: *My dick in your conscience*

**

Actual: *Eyreh be afass seder emmak*

Translation: *My dick in your mother's rib cage*

**

Actual: *Surmayye a'raasac*

Translation: *A shoe is on your head*

**

Actual: *Yela'an sabe'a jad lak*

Translation: *Damn your seventh grandfather*

Bulgarian Insults

Insults! Insults! 2nd Edition

Actual: *Gladna Karpatska valchitza s dalag kosam minet da ti prai deeba*

Translation: *Let a hungry Carpathian long-haired she-wolf blow your dick, fuck*

**

Actual: *Da eba taz kreeva neeva*

Translation: *Fuck this tilted field*

**

Actual: *Pederas grozen gyrbaw prokazhen*

Translation: *An unsightly hunchbacked leper queer*

**

Actual: *Mayka ti duha na mechki v gorata*

Translation: *Your mother sucks bears in the forest*

**

Actual: *Grozna si kato salata*

Translation: *You're as ugly as a salad*

**

Actual: *Nosa ti e kato ruska putka*

Translation: *Your nose is like a Russian pussy*

Irish Insults

Actual: *He's as thick as a bull's walt*

Translation: *As dense as an erect bull penis*

**

Actual: *Go n-ithe an cat thu, is go n-ithe an diabhal an cat*

Translation: *May the cat eat you, and may the devil eat the cat*

Chinese Insults

Actual: *Cao ni zu zong shi ba dai*

Translation: *Fuck the 18 generations of your ancestors*
**

Actual: *Nide muchin shr ega da wukwei*

Translation: *Your mother is a big turtle (essentially, they're calling your mother a whore)*

Icelander Insults

Actual: *Afatottari*

Translation: *Grandfather Fucker*
**

Actual: *Rollurioari*

Translation: *Sheepfucker*
**

Actual: *Naridill*

Translation: *Corpsefucker*
**

Actual: *Frandseroir*

Translation: *Unclefucker*

Insults! Insults! 2ⁿᵈ Edition

**

Actual: *Drullusukkor*

Translation: *Plunger (plumbing tool)*

Armenian Insults

Actual: *Dzvis ty*

Translation: *My nut's twin*

**

Actual: *Eshu Koorak*

Translation: *Son of Donkey*

**

Actual: *Eshoon noor oodel chi vayeler*

Translation: *It's not pretty watching a jackass try to eat a pomegranate (klutz)*

**

Actual: *Krisnera zhazh tan vred*

Translation: *Let the rats cum on you*

**

Actual: *Kak oudelic shoon*

Translation: *Shit eating dog.*

**

Actual: Glirit mortin hed sarma shinem

Translation: *I'll make sarma from your foreskin*

Serbian Insults

Actual: *Jebo ti jeza u ledja*

Translation: *May you fuck a hedgehog*

**

Actual: *Popasi me chmarne*

Translation: *Graze on my ass hair*

**

Actual: *Jebo te Papa*

Translation: *The Pope fucks you*

**

Actual: *Da bog da trazio detzoo Gaygerovim broyachem*

Translation: *May God lend you a Geiger counter to find your children with*

Malay Insults

Actual: *Da Bog da ti zena rodila stonogu pa ceo zivot radio za cipele*

Translation: *May your wife give birth to a centipede so you have to work for shoes all your life*

**

Actual: *Boon chon doi (read: Boon chon doh-yee)*

Translation: *Essentially, this refers to a man who walks behind his boss and holds his balls up for him.*

Insults! Insults! 2ⁿᵈ Edition

**

Actual: *Da bog da ti kuca bila na CNN-U*

Translation: *May your house be live on CNN (may your house be bombed)*

**

Actual: *Da bi te majka prepoznala u bureku*

Translation: *Let your mother recognize you in a meat pie*

Swahili Insult

Actual: *Una tombwa na punda (read: Ooh-na tom-bwah na poon-dah)*

Translation: *You are being fucked by a donkey*

Filipino Insults

Actual: *Putangina mo*

Translation: *Your mother is a whore*

**

Actual: *Hindot ka*

Translation: *you fuckhead or fuck you*

**

Actual: *Pukingina mo*

Translation: *cunt of your mother*

**

Actual: *Tae mo*

Insults! Insults! 2nd Edition

Translation: *shithead*

**

Actual: *Pesteng ulupong*

Translation: *you accursed snake*

One Word Insults

Sometimes, one word is enough. You're probably familiar with these one-word insults, some of which have been peppered throughout the book. Some of the most common include 'fuck', 'fucker', and 'idiot' – but do you realize there's actually more? In fact, there are one-word insults coming from different languages, and you'd find that they can be so much more creative – not to mention have richer meanings. Following are other one-word insults that your friend or enemy – will find offensive.

- Dickhead
- Ass Kisser
- Airhead
- Bimbo
- Deadbeat
- Fruitcake
- Geezer
- Lardass
- Loudmouth

Insults! Insults! 2nd Edition

- Tightass
- Tightarse
- Scumbag
- Wanker (British) - idiot
- Yokel
- Zero
- Tosser (British) – asshole
- Slag (British) – whore
- Barmy (British) – crazy
- Git (British) – moron
- Gormless (British) – no common sense
- Minger (British) – incredibly unappealing female
- Prat (British) – idiot
- Trollop (British) – whore
- Uphill Gardener (British) – homosexual
- Knob (British) – dick
- Ligger (British) – freeloader
- Plug-Ugly (British) – very ugly person

Insults for Intelligent People

Have you ever found yourself in polite company but badly wanting to insult someone? You can insult them to their face with a fairly complicated word that they obviously never hear of and imagine that sweet, sweet moment when they do an internet search and find out how insulting it was. Well, here are some of the words you can use to make this dream happen! A list of complicated, scientific-sounding words that insult people before they realize they've been insulted!

- *Microphallus – calling someone this essentially means he has a very small penis*

- *Cacafuego – someone who loves to boast or brag about anything and everything under the sun*

- *Buncombe – equivalent to bullshit, this is the word you use when you know someone is lying to you*

- *Corpulent – someone who is very, very fat*

- *Bescumber – the word means: to spray with poo*

- *Hircismus – this refers to someone with a terrible smell from their armpit*

- *Maladroit – equivalent to: klutz or someone who is very clumsy*

- *Feist – this one can have different meanings. It can be used to refer to someone who has very little worth, or someone with a dubious ancestry, a mongrel*

One thing to keep in mind about one-word insults is that they vary from one person to another. For example, a black person might feel insulted when called 'nigger' by a white person, but a black person saying the same thing won't probably end up offending anyone.

Who to Insult?

Insults! Insults! 2nd Edition

After reading this book, you've been given a full arsenal of ready insults to use against, well, practically anyone. Obviously, you can start trying them out one by one – but who should you insult? Ideally, you should only insult people you don't like because delivering some of these comebacks might lose you one, two, or even all your friends. Of course, perhaps you're in the kind of friendship wherein insults like these are just shrugged off – good for you!

To maximize the impact of your insult, rely largely on timing and the person you're trying to insult. To top it off, here's how to make the most out of body language:

- Use the most derogatory voice you can manage. Your tone actually depends largely on the type of insult you're trying to make. Typically, a dry, sarcastic tone would work best because it makes you seem nonchalant even while spearing your opponent's ego with a well-placed comeback.

- Don't forget the eyes – this can be incredibly powerful when it comes to insults. A sarcastic, all-encompassing sweep of the eyes can make a person feel more ashamed and therefore, more conscious of the insult you're about to give. This is especially true for fat people, women, or basically anyone who has negative attributes that are out in the open.

- In some cases, a twitch of your lips may also work – this is what most people would call a 'sneer'. This usually comes with the full-body swipe you do with your eyes.

- Keep in mind that the best insults are given quickly and decisively. Like jokes, if you have to explain an insult to others, then it isn't really much of an insult.

REMEMBER!

Insulting is an art and much like with delivering jokes, it must be done under the right circumstances – in this case, with the right timing. Sure, you may hurt someone's feelings – but that's the whole point of insulting a person, right? That being said, it's a good idea to attack where the person is most vulnerable, hence the insults for stupid people, fat people, girls, guys, and even people from different cultures! Everything is fair game – just make sure that you're prepared to deal with the consequences of the insult.

Remember, you can be insulted as well and it might also hurt – especially if the other person is perfectly aware of your vulnerability. In some cases, be prepared for a physical confrontation – it's the price you pay for being well versed when it comes to insults.

Those being said, have fun!

Conclusion

Thank you again for purchasing this book!

I hope this book was able to help you to learn awesome insults as well as useful information on how you can give insults like a *master*.

The next step is to try practicing these with your friends and learn how to come up with your own insults.

Finally, if you enjoyed this book, please take the time to share your thoughts and post a review on Amazon. We do our best to reach out to readers and provide the best value we can. Your positive review will help us achieve that. It'd be greatly appreciated!

Thank you and good luck!

Insults! Insults! 2nd Edition

Check Out My Other Books

Below you'll find some of my other popular books that are popular on Amazon and Kindle as well. Simply click on the links below to check them out. Alternatively, you can visit my author page on Amazon to see other work done by me.

151 Hilarious Knock Knock Jokes Ever

http://amzn.to/1iexRea

If the links do not work, for whatever reason, you can simply search for these titles on the Amazon website to find them.

Printed in Great Britain
by Amazon